THE CAT IN THE HAT
Knows a Lot About That!™

Wings and Paws
and
Fins and Claws

Written by Tish Rabe · Illustrated by Aristides Ruiz

A GOLDEN BOOK · NEW YORK

TM and copyright © by Dr. Seuss Enterprises, L.P. 2010. All rights reserved. Published in the United States by Golden Books, an imprint of Random House Children's Books, a division of Random House, Inc., 1745 Broadway, New York, NY 10019. Golden Books, A Golden Book, and the G colophon are registered trademarks of Random House, Inc.

Based in part on *The Cat in the Hat Knows a Lot About That!* TV series © CITH Productions, Inc. (a subsidiary of Portfolio Entertainment, Inc.), and Red Hat Animation, Ltd. (a subsidiary of Collingwood O'Hare Productions, Ltd.), 2010–2011.

THE CAT IN THE HAT KNOWS A LOT ABOUT THAT! logo and word mark TM 2010 Dr. Seuss Enterprises, L.P., Portfolio Entertainment, Inc., and Collingwood O'Hare Productions, Ltd. All rights reserved. The PBS KIDS logo is a registered trademark of PBS. Both are used with permission. All rights reserved.

Broadcast in Canada by Treehouse™. Treehouse™ is a trademark of the Corus® Entertainment Inc. group of companies. All rights reserved.

Visit us on the Web!
www.randomhouse.com/kids
Seussville.com
pbskids.org/catinthehat
treehousetv.com

ISBN: 978-0-375-85928-1
Printed in the United States of America
10 9 8 7 6 5 4 3 2 1

We're off in the Thinga-ma-jigger today!

We'll see flowers and animals and insects—hooray!

A hummingbird's swift because of its size.

Its quick-beating wings sound a hum when it flies.

This robin appears on the first day of spring.

A fat, juicy worm is his favorite thing.

This duck likes to nest in the rushes onshore.

She lays three eggs and sometimes more.

Look closely at this picture and at the one on the next page.
Can you find four things that are different there?

ANSWER:

In the dark of the night, an owl can see!

Her owlets are safe in a nest in a tree.

This bright parakeet so likes to sing.

She sits in her cage on her favorite swing.

How many times can you find the word *parakeet* ?
Look up, down, backward, and forward.

```
P S A I P N C H P O Z
K Y T O E N O R A F P
A S R P U H C L R H W
N R A K T Z T J A R K
A E D I Y H E H K A T
P A R A K E E T E H A
U S W I T H K H E T T
T A D R E Y A E T O E
M S Z I T L R N G F E
A S T E E K A R A P T
U O D Q T H P H G O I
```

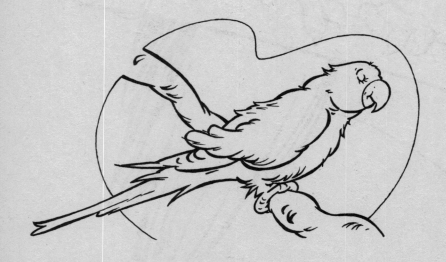

Draw a line to the shadow that matches each bird.

The spoonbill lives in a damp lagoon.

Its bill is shaped just like a spoon!

This toucan's beak is big as can be.

It's handy for picking fruit from a tree.

Help the toucan find her way to the rain forest.

Circle the bird that is different.

A

B

C

D

E

A woodpecker's beak is sharp and strong.

The nightingale has a most haunting song.

A chickadee's call sounds like "chick-a-dee-dee."

Sally finds a nest of them up in a tree.

Can you help Nick find the bird that hums?

What kind of bird is this? Connect the dots and find out!

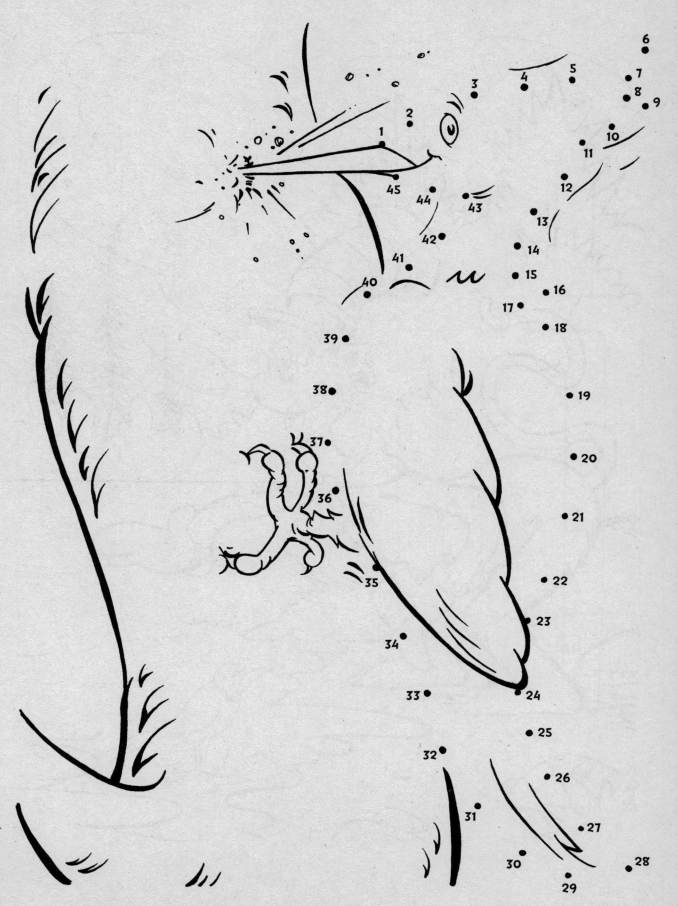

Plovers can live beside a lake.

He scans the water for fish to take.

Sandpipers run with the waves at low tide.

They search with their bills to find worms where they hide.

This seagull is playing a sneaky trick.

Hey! Look out for your picnic, Sally and Nick!

Help the chickadee get back to her nest.

START

FINISH

ANSWER:

Draw a picture of your favorite bird in this tree.

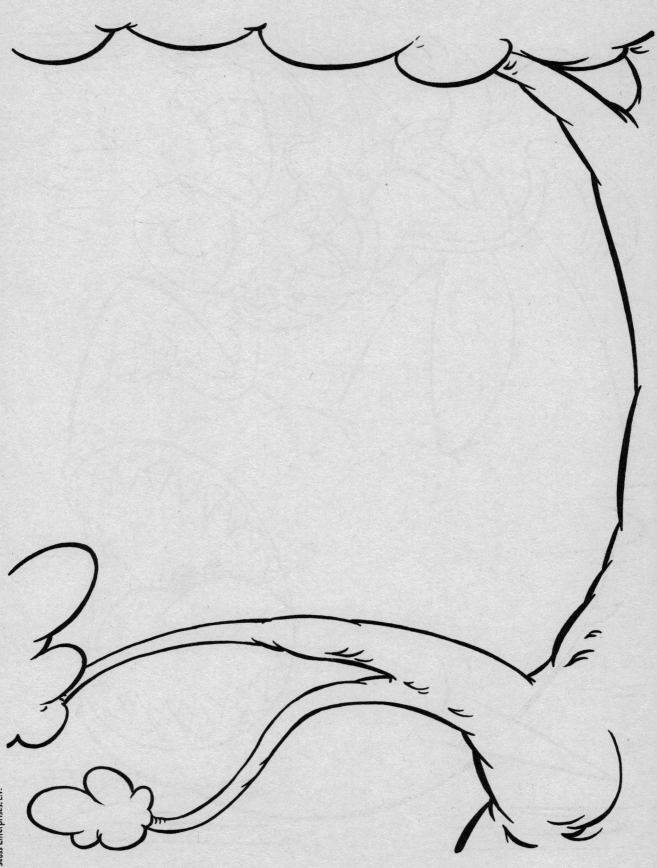

Neat rows of teeth grow in a shark's face.

When the front row wears out, the next row takes its place.

Manatees are mammals, like you and like me.

They have lungs and give milk to their babies, you see.

The blue whale weighs tons, maybe ninety or more.

It's bigger than even a big dinosaur.

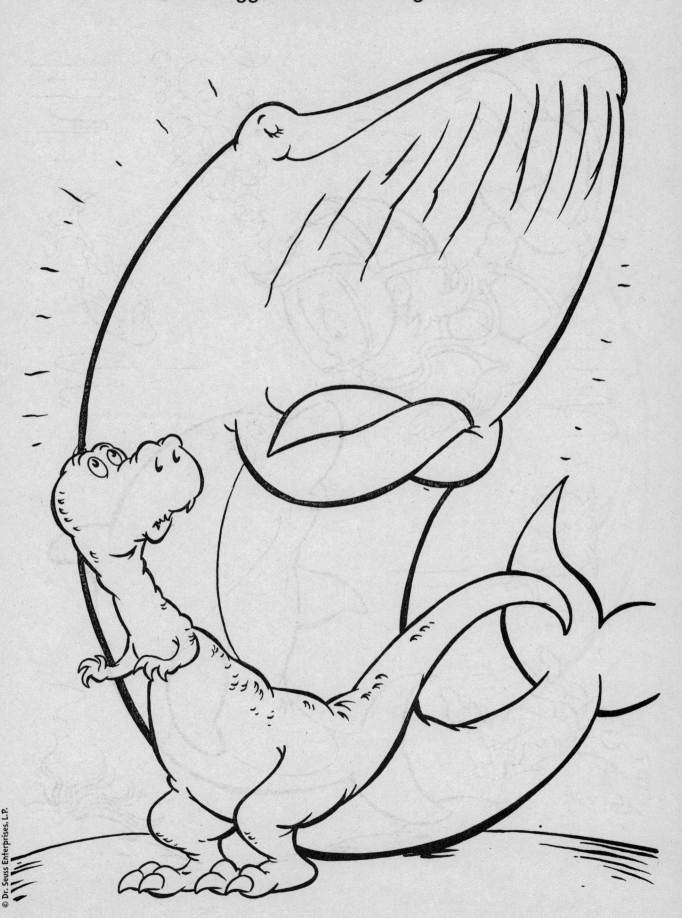

Because it is smallish, the porpoise is shy.

It swims near the shore and does not leap up high.

The jellyfish is a most interesting fella.

He looks kind of like a transparent umbrella!

Help the baby manatee find its mother.

START

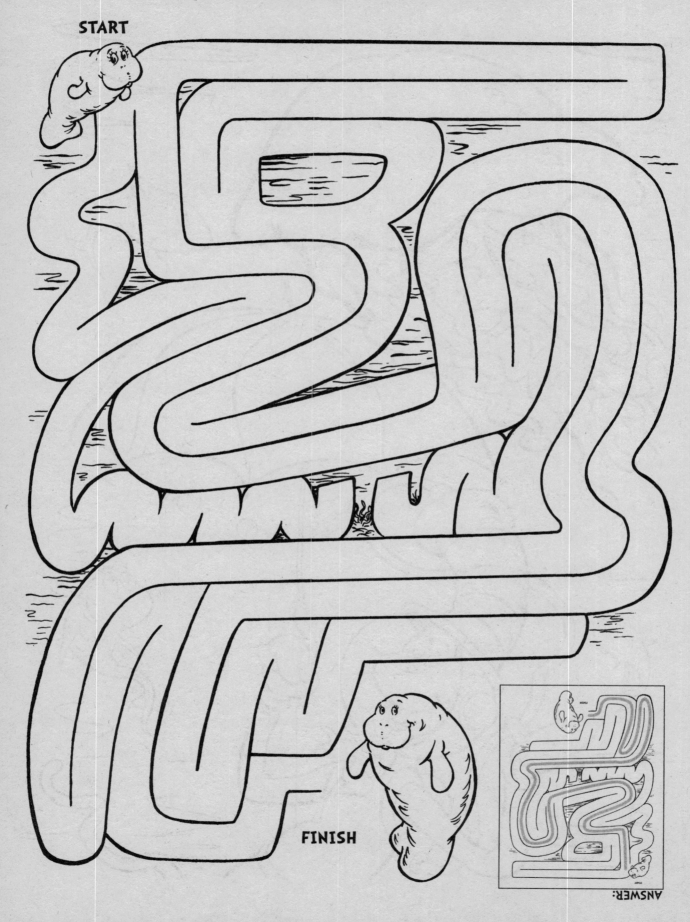

FINISH

ANSWER:

Circle the five teeth this shark has lost.

This is a dogfish, but he never barks.

Here is a pair of striped tiger sharks.

These silvery salmon shine in the sun.

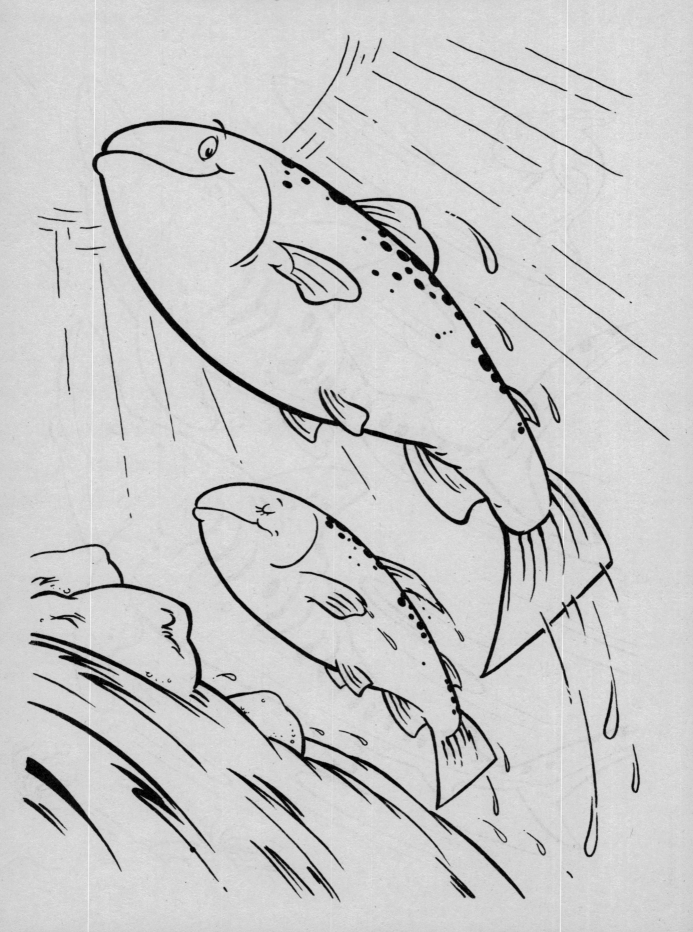

This bear cub is hoping that he can catch one!

This guinea pig is furry and cute.

It nibbles on vegetables and fresh fruit.

In the desert, fox kits sleep all day.

At night, the kits come out to play.

The giraffe has horns upon its head.

But reindeer and moose have antlers instead.

An impala likes to leap—that's called "pronking."

An elephant makes a noise that sounds like honking.

This panda likes to chew bamboo.

Thing One wants some bamboo, too.

Help the fox kit find her way to her brother and sister.

Which two pictures of the elephant are exactly the same?

ANSWER: B and D.

A sea otter naps wrapped in kelp all day.

The kelp keeps the otter from floating away.

How did the horseshoe crab get its name?

Its shell and a horseshoe are both shaped the same.

There are over thirty thousand kinds of snails.

Thing One and Thing Two need bigger pails!

Sea urchins like this one are covered in spines.

They look a lot like porcupines!

Help Thing One and Thing Two count all the snails.
How many are there?

Draw a line from each picture to its close-up.

Here is an army of leaf-cutting ants.

They chew the leaves right off the plants.

This male cricket sings and sings.

He makes his music by rubbing his wings.

On warm summer evenings, you see a light.

Fireflies flash on and off in the night.

A grasshopper has five eyes in all . . .

This little lizard has a great big frill.

Will it scare off enemies? Yes, it will!

This hungry chameleon snaps up a fly.

It grabs a moth as it flies by.

Help Thing Two count all the reptiles on this page.

What is this reptile's name?
Use *A*, *E*, *I*, *O*, or *U* to find out!

CH_M_L___N

ANSWER: Chameleon.

Crocodiles have big teeth and strong legs.

Crocodile babies hatch from eggs.

Find and circle three birds, three reptiles, three flowers, and three insects.

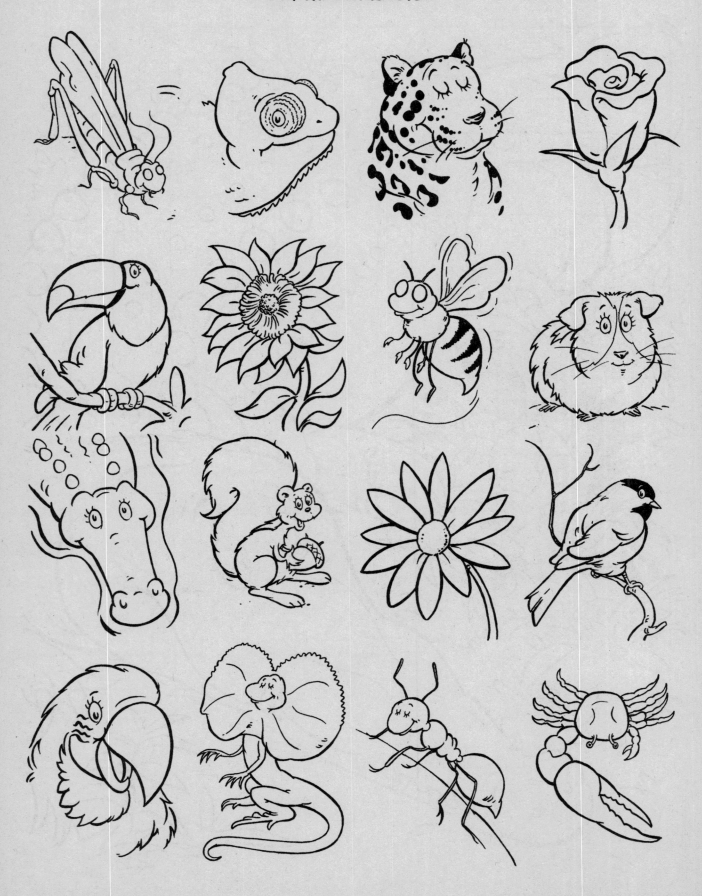

Sally is looking for the crocodile's nest.
Can you help her find it?

START

FINISH

ANSWER:

In the Thinga-ma-jigger, we can always see . . .

... the wonders of nature. Come fly with me!

Draw a picture of the Thinga-ma-jigger here.

THINGA-MA-JIGGER